THE HUMAN BODY

THE SKELETAL SYSTEM

By Greg Roza

Gareth Stevens
Publishing

Please visit our website, www.garethstevens.com. For a free color catalog of all our high-quality books, call toll free 1-800-542-2595 or fax 1-877-542-2596.

Library of Congress Cataloging-in-Publication Data

Roza, Greg.
The skeletal system / Greg Roza.
    p. cm. — (The human body)
Includes index.
ISBN 978-1-4339-6598-2 (pbk.)
ISBN 978-1-4339-6599-9 (6-pack)
ISBN 978-1-4339-6596-8 (library binding)
1. Human skeleton—Juvenile literature. 2. Human skeleton—Growth—Juvenile literature. I. Title.
QM101.R69 2012
612.7'51—dc23

                              2011036635

First Edition

Published in 2012 by
Gareth Stevens Publishing
111 East 14th Street, Suite 349
New York, NY 10003

Copyright © 2012 Gareth Stevens Publishing

Designer: Daniel Hosek
Editor: Greg Roza

Photo credits: Cover, p. 1 Science Picture Co./Science Faction/Getty Images; all backgrounds, pp. 5, 9 (all images), 13, 15 (all images), 16–17 (all images), 20–21 (all images), 23, 27 (arthritis inset), 28–29 (all images) Shutterstock.com; p. 7 (skeleton) Medical Images/Universal Images Group/Getty Images; p. 7 (ear inset) MedicalRF.com/ Getty Images; pp. 10–11 Dorling Kindersley/The Agency Collection/Getty Images; p. 19 Steve Gschmeissner/Science Photo Library/Getty Images; p. 25 Don Farrall/Photodisc/ Getty Images; p. 27 (main image) Nucleus Medical Arts/Visuals Unlimited/Getty Images.

Printed in the United States of America

CPSIA compliance information: Batch #CW12GS: For further information contact Gareth Stevens, New York, New York at 1-800-542-2595.

Contents

Words in the glossary appear in **bold** type
the first time they are used in the text.

The Skeleton Inside You

Think about what your life would be like without bones. You'd just be a big blob on the floor! You wouldn't be able to run, stand up, or move at all. But that's not all. Without bones, you wouldn't be able to hear, you wouldn't have blood, and your tongue wouldn't work properly! In short, you couldn't live without your bones.

You've probably seen skeletons on Halloween, or maybe you've seen one hanging in your science classroom. When you were born, you had about 300 bones! However, as you grew, some of them fused, or grew together. An adult body contains 206 bones. That includes three tiny bones in each ear. Altogether, these bones make up the skeletal system.

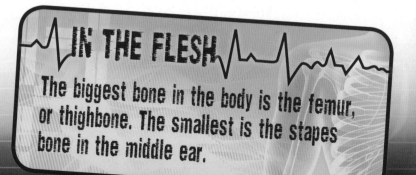

IN THE FLESH

The biggest bone in the body is the femur, or thighbone. The smallest is the stapes bone in the middle ear.

vertebrae

scapula

carpals

femur

FOUR KINDS OF BONES

Bones are placed into four groups based on their shape. Long bones, such as the femur in the leg, support weight or act as a **lever**. Short bones, such as the carpals of the hand, provide support but little movement. Flat bones, such as the scapula (shoulder blade), protect organs and provide a large area for muscles to attach to. Irregular bones have odd shapes, like the vertebrae of the backbone.

Bones of the Body

The skeletal system has two main groups of bones. The axial skeleton is composed of the skull, spine, ribs, and sternum (breastbone). These bones form the axis, or central supportive structure, of the body.

The skull is made up of 22 bones. The eight flat bones of the **cranium** fit together like puzzle pieces. The 14 irregular facial bones attach tightly to the cranial bones. The skull bones protect the brain and sense organs. Teeth are rooted in the two jaw bones. The six ear bones are within the skull, although they aren't part of it.

The spine supports the skull and ribs. It also protects the **spinal cord**. The ribs and sternum form the main structure of the human trunk, or torso, and protect the heart and lungs.

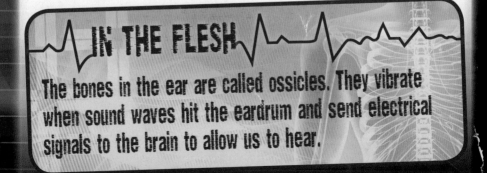

IN THE FLESH

The bones in the ear are called ossicles. They vibrate when sound waves hit the eardrum and send electrical signals to the brain to allow us to hear.

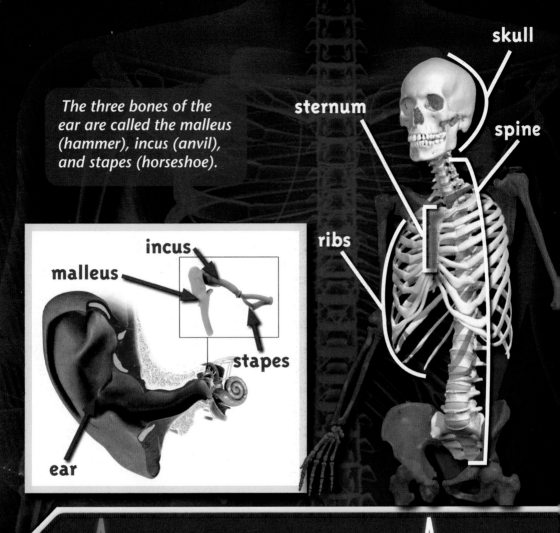

The three bones of the ear are called the malleus (hammer), incus (anvil), and stapes (horseshoe).

incus

malleus

stapes

ear

sternum

skull

spine

ribs

THE SPINE AND VERTEBRAE

The spine is made up of a chain of 33 irregular bones called vertebrae. They surround the spinal cord somewhat like beads on a string. Many bones and muscles connect to the vertebrae. The vertebrae form curves as they go down. The top vertebra, the atlas, supports the skull. The bottom section of the spine—the coccyx or tailbone—is made up of three to five increasingly smaller vertebrae that are fused together.

The appendicular skeleton is the more moveable part of the skeletal system. It's composed of two main sections that attach to the spinal column by way of "girdles." The pectoral girdle is made up of two clavicles (collarbones) and two scapulas (shoulder blades). It supports the bones of the arms and hands. The pelvic girdle is the pelvis. It supports the bones of the legs and feet.

The bones of the arms and legs are similar. Ball-and-socket joints connect the humerus (upper arm bone) to the scapula and the femur (thighbone) to the pelvis. The humerus and femur are two of the strongest bones in the body. The radius and ulna run from the elbow to the hand. The tibia and fibula run from the knee to the foot.

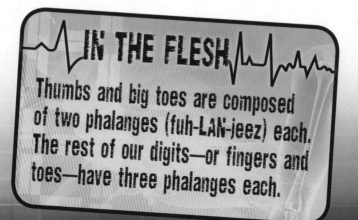

IN THE FLESH

Thumbs and big toes are composed of two phalanges (fuh-LAN-jeez) each. The rest of our digits—or fingers and toes—have three phalanges each.

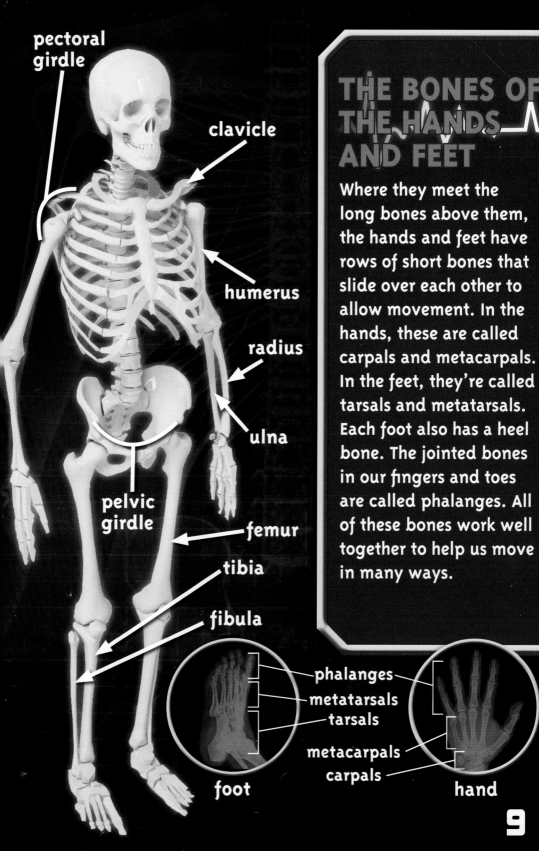

pectoral girdle

clavicle

humerus

radius

ulna

pelvic girdle

femur

tibia

fibula

Where they meet the long bones above them, the hands and feet have rows of short bones that slide over each other to allow movement. In the hands, these are called carpals and metacarpals. In the feet, they're called tarsals and metatarsals. Each foot also has a heel bone. The jointed bones in our fingers and toes are called phalanges. All of these bones work well together to help us move in many ways.

phalanges

metatarsals

tarsals

metacarpals

carpals

foot

hand

9

Bone Matter

Bones may seem solid, but they're not. The outer layer, called the cortex, is made out of compact bone, which is smooth and very hard. It's what we see when we look at a skeleton. The tissue in compact bone is pressed tightly together, which is where it gets its name. Narrow channels carrying nerves and blood vessels run through compact bone.

compact bone

cancellous bone

periosteum

bone marrow

Compact bone is also called cortical bone. This comes from the word "cortex."

Inside the compact bone is cancellous bone. It's made up of a network of crisscrossing pieces of bone called trabeculae (truh-BEH-kyuh-lee). This network may look **fragile**, but it's actually very strong. The trabeculae line up to give the bone the best support, kind of like the rafters inside a roof. The center of many bones contains a substance called marrow, which we'll discuss later.

IN THE FLESH

Bones are surrounded by a thin layer of tissue called periosteum (pehr-ee-AHS-tee-uhm). This covering contains blood vessels and nerves.

WHAT'S IN OUR BONES?

Bones consist of four kinds of cells. Osteoblasts make new bone and help repair damaged bones. Osteocytes take in nutrients from blood vessels and get rid of waste. Osteoclasts build up and break down bone tissue. Stem cells don't do anything until they're needed. Then they become osteoblasts. The rest is nonliving materials, such as the minerals calcium, phosphorus, and sodium, and a protein called collagen. These materials help make bones hard and strong.

The Meeting Place

The area where two or more bones meet is called a joint. Most joints are synovial (suh-NOH-vee-uhl). They allow us to move our body and absorb shocks. A synovial joint, such as the knee, is surrounded by a sac called the joint **capsule**. It's lined with a special tissue that makes synovial fluid, which acts as a **lubricant** to allow the joints to bend and flex easily. A special type of **cartilage** connects and cushions the bones that meet inside the capsule.

Another kind of joint, such as those in the pelvis and between the vertebrae of the spine, allows limited movement. The joints of the skull are a third kind. They don't move at all. However, these joints start soft and allow the skull bones to grow during childhood.

IN THE FLESH

Ligaments are strong but flexible cords that fasten bones together around the joints.

muscle

tendon

bone

cartilage

synovial fluid

MOVING JOINTS

The human skeleton has four main kinds of synovial joints. Ball-and-socket joints like the hip and shoulder allow for the most movement. Saddle joints, such those found in the thumbs, allow back-and-forth and up-and-down movement. Elbows and knees are hinge joints. They allow back-and-forth movement in one direction. Plane joints, such as those between the metacarpal bones in the hand, allow limited sliding motions.

Support and Movement

The skeletal system forms the frame that supports the human body. Without it, we'd just be a pile of jelly! The body's muscles and organs are anchored to the skeletal system, providing them with support. This holds the body together and gives it shape. The spine is the body's main support structure. All the bones connect to it directly or through other bones, and it allows us to stand upright.

The bones and joints work with our muscles and allow us to move in many different ways. Many bones act as levers to help move objects. Our bones allow us to walk, jump, and throw. But they also allow us to complete more delicate actions, such as writing and speaking.

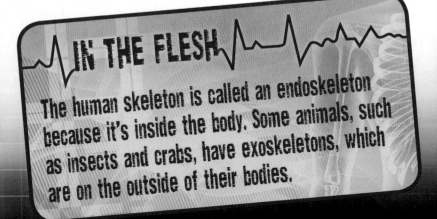

IN THE FLESH

The human skeleton is called an endoskeleton because it's inside the body. Some animals, such as insects and crabs, have exoskeletons, which are on the outside of their bodies.

HYOID BONE

The hyoid is a horseshoe-shaped bone. It's located at the top of the neck just below the jaw bone. The hyoid is the only bone not directly connected to any other bones. It's held in place by muscles and tendons. However, it provides an anchor point for the muscles of the tongue. The hyoid helps with chewing and swallowing. It also works with the tongue and larynx, or voice box, to produce speech.

hyoid bone

Protection

Many bones protect important tissues and organs. The bones of the skull form a shell around the brain and top of the spinal column. They also give some protection to the eyes, nose, and mouth.

The lungs, heart, and other organs are protected by the sternum and the ribs. Together, these bones form the rib cage. The sternum is a thick, T-shaped bone in the center of the chest. Twenty-four ribs, 12 on each side, begin at the spine and curve around toward the sternum. Cartilage joins all but the bottom two ribs on each side to the sternum.

The vertebrae of the spine protect the spinal cord. The vertebrae are connected by round pieces of cartilage commonly called disks, which allow them to flex and move.

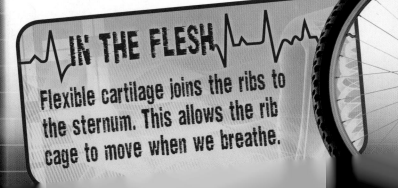

IN THE FLESH

Flexible cartilage joins the ribs to the sternum. This allows the rib cage to move when we breathe.

The skull is somewhat like a helmet under your hair! However, we still need to wear a real helmet when riding a bike to keep our skull from being damaged during falls.

^SESAMOID BONES

Sesamoid bones are short or irregular bones that are **embedded** within and held in place by tendons. Sesamoid bones protect joints. The patella, or kneecap, is the largest sesamoid bone in the body. It protects the synovial joint of the knee. The petellar tendon keeps it in place. Other sesamoid bones can be found in the metacarpals of the hands and the metatarsals of the feet.

patella

Factories and Storehouses

Bones do more than provide structure, support, and protection. They play an important role in the production of cells in the body. They're also an important storehouse for minerals.

Human bones are blood factories! The center of many bones contains a jelly-like substance called bone marrow. There are two types of bone marrow—red and yellow. Red marrow creates blood cells. Red blood cells carry oxygen to organs throughout the body. White blood cells help fight illnesses. Along with the liver and spleen, red marrow also helps destroy old red blood cells.

Fat is stored in yellow marrow. However, the body can change yellow marrow into red marrow under certain conditions—for example, in case of serious blood loss.

IN THE FLESH

From birth to about age 7, all marrow is red. In adults, red marrow is found in the vertebrae, hips, rib cage, skull, and at the ends of the long bones of the arms and legs.

This image was made with a special microscope. It shows red and white blood cells in human bone marrow.

STEM CELLS

Stem cells are part of an important repair system for the human body. They're capable of replacing damaged or worn-out cells. Scientists study stem cells to find out how the body repairs itself. Bone marrow contains stem cells. These cells produce new cells by dividing. Some new cells continue as stem cells. Other new cells become different types of blood cells. This is how the bones replace old blood cells.

Blood vessels run throughout the bones, allowing blood to flow into and out of them. The blood cells marrow makes pass through the blood vessels and into the rest of the body. The blood vessels also allow the body to send excess minerals to the bones for later use.

The two most common minerals in the body are calcium and phosphorus. They're very important to the way the body functions. Cells use these minerals during chemical reactions. The minerals also help keep our bones and teeth strong. When there's too much calcium or phosphorus in the bloodstream, the excess is stored in the bones for future use. When there's not enough of these minerals in the bloodstream, they're released by the bones.

Dairy foods—such as milk and cheese—are a good source of calcium. Beef, nuts, and chocolate contain phosphorus.

PART OF THE ENDOCRINE SYSTEM

Scientists have discovered that the bones are part of the endocrine system. This system is made up of organs called glands that make chemicals called hormones. Hormones are chemicals that affect the way our bodies function. Bones make the hormone osteocalcin, which helps make our bones strong. Osteocalcin also helps control the body's use of sugar and controls where fat is stored in the body. Scientists think osteocalcin may be used to fight diabetes in the future.

IN THE FLESH

Osteocalcin is made by osteoblast cells in the bones.

Male and Female Skeletons

Although the skeletons of men and women look very similar, they have several key differences. Generally speaking, male bones are heavier and longer. Female bones finish developing around age 18. Male bones finish developing around age 21.

Male and female skulls look different. Male skulls have larger, stronger features. Brow ridges, for example, are generally larger in male skulls. Male chins are usually more square. Female chins are more rounded and narrow.

The biggest differences between male and female skeletons can be seen in the pelvis. The largest parts of the pelvis, called the ilia, are wider in female skeletons. The space between the two halves of the pelvis is wider in women than in men. The tailbone is more moveable in female skeletons, too. These differences allow women to give birth.

IN THE FLESH

The formation of bone tissue is called ossification.

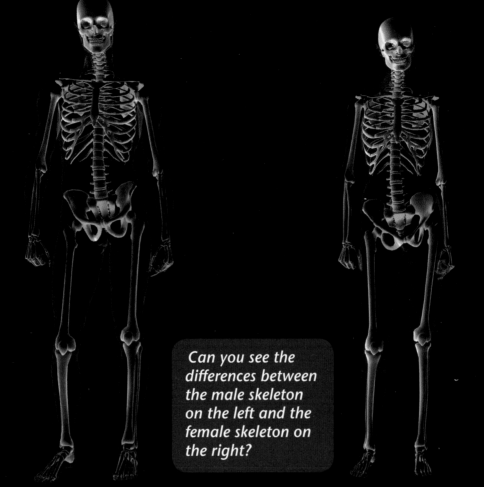

Can you see the differences between the male skeleton on the left and the female skeleton on the right?

GROWING BONES

Male and female bones are nearly identical at birth. A newborn's bones are soft and flexible. Most are very similar to cartilage. Even the bones of the skull are soft. As a child grows, its bones harden. In women, the hormone estrogen causes the bones to finish growing earlier than in men. In men, the hormone testosterone gives the bones more time to develop, allowing them to achieve greater length and mass.

Bone Injuries and Disorders

Our bones are very tough. However, when enough pressure is placed on them, they can bruise or break. There are different kinds of fractures, or breaks. A hairline fracture is a minor break that's often missed on an X-ray. A comminuted fracture occurs when a bone breaks into three or more pieces. An open fracture occurs when part of the bone pierces the skin. Skull fractures can be particularly dangerous because there's a risk the brain will be damaged.

Injuries to the spine can be very dangerous, too. Many spine injuries involve the flexible disks between the vertebrae. These disks can become damaged or break down over time, leading to recurring pain or life-threatening complications.

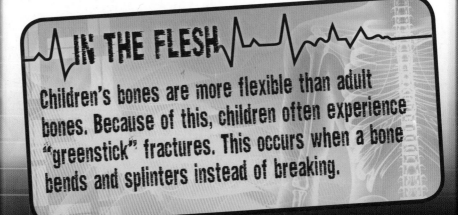

IN THE FLESH

Children's bones are more flexible than adult bones. Because of this, children often experience "greenstick" fractures. This occurs when a bone bends and splinters instead of breaking.

JOINT INJURIES

A sprain is an injury to the ligament around a joint. It can happen when a ligament is stretched too far or when it tears. Many athletes sprain their ankles. A dislocation occurs when the ends of two bones are forced apart. This can cause damage to ligaments, nerves, and blood vessels. Sprains and dislocations cause pain and swelling. Minor joint injuries heal with rest, but major injuries sometimes require surgery.

This X-ray shows the screws and plates required to fix a hip fracture.

There are several notable bone diseases, including **infections** and **cancer**. Osteoporosis is the most common bone disease. This illness is marked by a loss of bone **density** over time. It affects women more than men—about one in five women over the age of 50 in the United States has osteoporosis. Osteoporosis occurs when the body loses too much bone tissue or doesn't make enough. It results in brittle, weak bones. It can be prevented by increasing the amount of calcium in the diet.

Spina bifida is a birth defect that occurs when an unborn baby's spine doesn't form properly. The condition is often discovered and treated immediately after birth with surgery. Many people recover completely, while others require crutches or a wheelchair to get around.

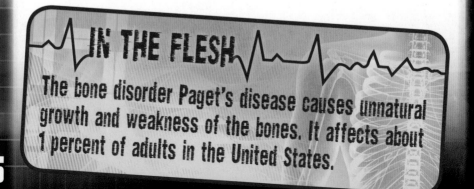

IN THE FLESH

The bone disorder Paget's disease causes unnatural growth and weakness of the bones. It affects about 1 percent of adults in the United States.

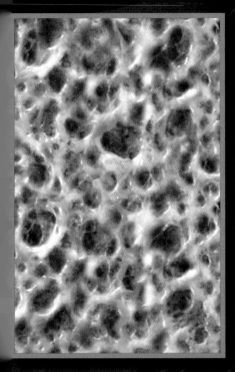

The picture above shows healthy bone. The picture below shows bone affected by osteoporosis.

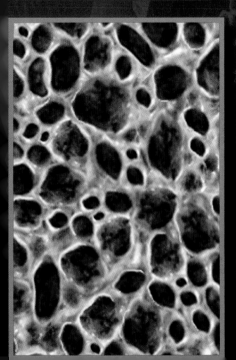

ARTHRITIS

Arthritis is painful swelling in one or more joints. Some kinds are caused by injuries or general usage over a long time. Other kinds are caused by infections or problems with the **immune system**. The most common form is called osteoarthritis. It's marked by the breakdown of cartilage between bones, which causes the bones to grind together. The joints become stiff, swollen, and painful. Some drugs help reduce pain, but there's no cure for arthritis.

Healthy Bones

Whether you're riding a bike, playing football, or skateboarding, it's important to protect your joints and bones. Always wear a helmet and protective pads on your knees, elbows, ribs, and shins. Bone and joint injuries that occur early in life can cause problems as we grow older.

It's important for children and teens to get plenty of calcium in their diet to help build strong bones. Adults reach peak bone mass in their early twenties. As we grow older, we can lose bone density. To maintain healthy bones, adults—and especially women—need to make sure they get enough calcium every day. In addition to calcium, lifting weights regularly helps develop and maintain healthy bones. Taking care of your bones as you grow older will help them take care of you!

Calcium!
THE BONE-BUILDING MINERAL

Foods That Contain Calcium

Food	Serving Size	Calcium per Serving
low-fat yogurt, plain	8 oz	415 mg
cheddar cheese	1.5 oz	306 mg
nonfat milk (skim)	8 oz	296 mg
low-fat yogurt, with fruit	8 oz	313-384 mg
pink salmon, canned with bone	3 oz	181 mg
cottage cheese (1% milk fat)	1 cup	138 mg
spinach, cooked	0.5 cup	123 mg
frozen yogurt, vanilla	0.5 cup	103 mg
ice cream, vanilla	0.5 cup	84 mg
raw broccoli	0.5 cup	21 mg

Daily Requirements of Calcium

Age	Male	Female
0-6 months	200 mg	200 mg
7-12 months	260 mg	260 mg
1-3 years	700 mg	700 mg
4-8 years	1,000 mg	1,000 mg
9-18 years	1,300 mg	1,300 mg
19-50 years	1,000 mg	1,000 mg
51-70 years	1,000 mg	1,200 mg
71+ years	1,200 mg	1,200 mg

Glossary

cancer: a disease caused by the uncontrolled growth of cells in the body

capsule: a sac enclosing a body part

cartilage: tough, flexible tissue in the body

cranium: the part of the skull that covers the brain

density: the amount of a material in a given area

diabetes: a disorder that causes the body to produce excess urine and causes high levels of sugar in the blood

embedded: set solidly within something else

fragile: easily breakable

immune system: the parts of the body that fight germs and keep it healthy

infection: the spread of germs inside the body, causing illness

lever: a tool used to lift a load

lubricant: a substance that allows two surfaces to slide easily over each other, such as grease

spinal cord: a thick rope of nerve tissue extending from the brain

For More Information

BOOKS

Ballard, Carol. *What Happens to Broken Bones?* Chicago, IL: Raintree, 2011.

Burstein, John. *The Mighty Muscular and Skeletal Systems: How Do My Bones and Muscles Work?* New York, NY: Crabtree Publishing, 2009.

Macaulay, David. *The Way We Work: Getting to Know the Amazing Human Body.* Boston, MA: Houghton Mifflin, 2008.

WEBSITES

Bone Biology for Kids
depts.washington.edu/bonebio/
Find out more about your bones and how to care for them.

Your Bones
kidshealth.org/kid/htbw/bones.html
Read more about the human skeletal system.

Index